HABITATS OF THE WORLD

ISLANDS

ALISON BALLANCE

About Islands .2
Hawaii 4
Coconut Palms 6
Silverswords 8
Seabirds 10
Unusual Plants and Animals 12
   Lemurs 14
   Kiwis 16
   Giant Tortoises 18
   Komodo Dragons 20
Easter Island 22
Glossary 24
Index 24

DOMINIE PRESS
Pearson Learning Group

About Islands

An island is a piece of land surrounded by water. There are thousands of islands in oceans and lakes all around the world. An island can be as small as a tiny **coral atoll** or a rock. Greenland is the largest island in the world.

Hawaii

Many islands have been formed by **volcanoes**. The islands of Hawaii are the tops of undersea volcanoes. They are in the middle of the Pacific Ocean. The islands of Hawaii are so far away from any other land that they are the most **isolated** islands on Earth.

Coconut Palms

When it is first formed, an island is just bare rock. Over time, plants and animals arrive and make it their home. The coconut palm is a good traveler that has reached lots of islands. A coconut is a large seed that can float in the sea for months until it washes up on a beach and begins to grow.

Silverswords

This plant is called a silversword. Hawaii is home to many kinds of silverswords. Even though they may look different from each other, the silverswords are all related.

Seabirds

Islands are important places for seabirds. Seabirds live and feed at sea, but they must come **ashore** to breed. Lots of seabirds crowd onto islands to build nests and raise their **chicks**. During the breeding season, the islands are busy and noisy.

Unusual Plants and Animals

Islands are home to many strange and unusual plants and animals. This is an **ancient** kind of tree, which is now found only in New Caledonia.

Lemurs

Lemurs are distant relatives of monkeys and humans. They are found on only one island in the world—Madagascar, a large island off the coast of Africa. There are more than thirty different kinds of lemurs.

Kiwis

New Zealand has many **flightless** birds. The kiwi is a big, heavy bird that lives on the ground. Kiwis are **nocturnal**. They sleep during the day and hunt for worms at night.

Giant Tortoises

This giant tortoise lives on the Galapagos Islands. There are many kinds of Galapagos tortoises. Some of them are big and some are small, but they all came from one **species**. They eat grass and other plants.

Komodo Dragons

The biggest, fiercest hunter on the island of Komodo isn't a lion or a tiger—it is a lizard. The komodo dragon is a giant lizard. A komodo dragon can kill animals that are much bigger than itself.

Easter Island

The people of Easter Island destroyed everything that lived on their island. In the end, nothing was left except these statues. Islands are **precious** places. We should work hard to keep their unusual plants and animals alive.

GLOSSARY

ancient: Very, very old
ashore: On dry land
chicks: Baby birds, such as baby seabirds
coral atoll: A small island formed over a long time by the growth of coral
flightless: A bird that does not fly
isolated: Far away from anywhere else
nocturnal: An animal that is active during the night and sleeps during the day
precious: Something special that should be looked after
species: Types of animals that have something in common
volcanoes: Hills or mountains made up of hot rock that comes out of the ground and cools

INDEX

Africa, 15
ashore, 11
beach, 7
chicks, 11
coconut, 7
coconut palm, 7
coral atoll, 3
Easter Island, 23
Galapagos Islands, 19
Greenland, 3

Hawaii, 5, 9
kiwi(s), 17
Komodo, 21
komodo dragon, 21
lemurs, 15
lizard, 21
Madagascar, 15
monkeys, 15

nests, 11
New Caledonia, 13
New Zealand, 17
Pacific Ocean, 5
seabirds, 11
silversword(s), 9
statues, 23
tortoise(s), 19
volcano(es), 5